SENSES

Eating and tasting

Author's Note

I have worked alongside young children for more than 40 years. Over this period I have learned never to be surprised at their perceptive comments about the physical world in which they live. Many of their observations ('Have you seen the crinkles in the elephant's trunk?' 'How do seeds know which is their top and which is their bottom?') indicate keen observation and an intuitive use of the senses of taste, touch, sight, smell and hearing.

The sense-dependent nature of the young child should come as no surprise to parents and teachers. In the early years of life images provided by the senses shape our interpretation of our surroundings and lay the foundations upon which subsequent learning is built. The ideas of hot and cold, far and near, quiet and loud, sweet and sour, soft and hard are developed through the interaction of the child with his or her immediate environment. This interaction encourages observation and questioning which in turn leads to talk and the extension and deepening of language.

This book (like its companions in the series) is a picture book which seeks to encourage both looking and talking. The text may be read by child or adult. Alternatively it may be ignored, the pictures alone being used to trigger an exploration of the child's own insights.

Paperback edition published 2000

© Franklin Watts 1997
Franklin Watts
96 Leonard Street
London EC2A 4XD

Franklin Watts Australia
14 Mars Road
Lane Cove
NSW 2066

ISBN: 0 7496 2575 9 (Hbk)
         0 7496 3790 0 (Pbk)

A CIP catalogue record for this book
is available from the British Library.

Dewey Decimal Classification Number: 612.8

Editor: Sarah Snashall
Art Director: Robert Walster
Designer: Kirstie Billingham

Printed in Malaysia

Picture credits

Commissioned photography by Steve Shott: cover, 4, 5, 15, 22, 27.
Researched photography: The Anthony Blake Photo Library 9 (G. Buntrock), 12 (Rosenfeld), 18 (V. Watts), 20 (G. Buntrock), 23 (PFT Associates); Bruce Coleman 28 (N. Mcallister), 29 (J. Burton); Collections 17 (S. Lousada); The Image Bank 14 (S. Allen), 21 (J. Glenn); Rex Features 10 (H. T. Kaiser); Panos 24 (J. Dugast); Robert Harding 25, 26 (M. Chillmaid), 31; Spectrum Colour Library title page (C. Mauritius); Tony Stone 6 (B. Thomas), 11 (J. Koppel), 13 (L. Evans).

SENSES

Eating and tasting

by Henry Pluckrose

W
FRANKLIN WATTS
LONDON • SYDNEY

Everything we eat has a taste. Our sense of taste helps us to enjoy our food.

A human tongue
is covered with little taste buds.
These taste buds recognise
whether the food is sweet,
bitter, sour or salty.

Our sense of taste
works very closely
with our sense of smell.
The smell of food can
make us feel hungry.

What things do you like tasting?
The zesty taste
of a lemon,
or the sweet taste
of jelly beans?

Sometimes the way food
feels in our mouth
helps us to enjoy what we eat.
Nuts and crusty fresh bread
are crunchy and hard.
Newly baked biscuits
crumble in the mouth.

There are many words
to describe
how food feels to eat.
Apples are sharp and crisp,
berries are sweet and soft.

Some things taste best
when they are eaten cold . . .
ice-cream, fruit drinks, jelly.
When the weather is hot,
they help us to feel cool too!

Some foods like fish and chips
or burgers taste better
when they are eaten hot.
When the weather is cold
the heat of the food
warms us up!

We can change the taste of food
by cooking it in different ways.

Boiled potatoes
taste quite different from chips!

Some food
does not have to be cooked.
How many of these vegetables
have you eaten raw?

Even raw fish can taste good.

There are many different ways
of preparing food.
Around the world,
people enjoy spicy foods,
and foods with a very hot flavour.

In China and Japan
rice is an important food.
Sauces give each dish
a special taste.

Not everything is good to taste.
We clean our teeth
with toothpaste, not soap!

Many animals
have a sense of taste.
The snail tastes its food through
the two little horns (or tentacles)
on its head.
The grass snake tastes the air
with its forked tongue.

Without the sense of taste,
all our food
would taste the same . . .
perhaps as plain as water!

Investigations

This book has been prepared to encourage the young user to think about the sense of taste and the way in which we interpret the things we eat. Each picture spread creates an opportunity for talk. Sharing talk with a sympathetic adult plays an important part in the development of a child's understanding of the world. Through the subtlety of language, ideas are formed, questioned and developed.

The theme of taste might be explored through questions like these:

⭐ The sense of taste (pp 4-5). Describe a taste in words . . . how could you explain the taste of strawberries or ice cream to someone who had never tasted them? Using words in a purposeful way makes a significant contribution to language development.

⭐ The tongue (pp 6-7). Look at the surface of the tongue in a mirror. How does the surface of the tongue differ from that of the skin?

⭐ The interrelationship of the senses (pp 8-9). Discuss the relationship between the senses of taste and smell. Does the smell of something indicate how it might taste? (E.g. do things both smell and taste sweet – or sour or sharp?)

⭐ Preferences (pp 10-13). Make a personal list of tastes which the child likes and dislikes.

⭐ The mouth (pp 16-19). What other part of our mouths helps us to identify things which are hot or cold?

⭐ Cooking (pp 20-23). Cooking changes the way things taste. What things do we eat either raw or cooked? In what way does cooking alter the 'feel' of the food in our mouths?

⭐ Culture and food (pp 24-25). Explore the ways in which people of particular cultures prepare and present their food . . . and the ways in which they eat it . . . spoons, knives and forks, chopsticks.

⭐ Care of our bodies (pp 26-27). Stress the importance of oral hygiene – particularly cleaning teeth last thing at night. Why do we need to remove food deposits from our teeth?